LET'S TALK ABOUT LOVE

A Guide to Love and Come Alive
For the Awakening Mid- 30's Woman
Living with PTSD from Sexual Violence

Oscar Crawford

Oscar Crawford Media Publishing

Mesa, Arizona

Oscar Crawford Media
2242 East Harmony Avenue
Mesa, Arizona 85204

Copyright © 2018 Oscar Crawford
First Paperback Printing November 2018

ISBN 978-0-9677133-2-8

Originally Published in the USA by
Oscar Crawford Media Publishing, 2018

Printed in the USA

DEDICATION

I dedicate this book with love and affection for the mid – 30's woman awakening to self – love that suffered the indignity of rape as a child.

CONTENTS

ACKNOWLEDGEMENTS

I want to acknowledge my family that honored husband, father, and grandfather is a writer focused on helping people heal from their hurts and prepare for love. Thank you for being supportive Bonnie Crawford, Micha Goudeau, Makayla Hyman and Leia Goudeau.

Second, I want to thank an extensive list of personal special friends in my local and global orbit that have given of themselves to help me produce Let's Talk About Love. I also want to thank one very special healer, Stephanie Gregory. I forever honor all of you with my love and gratitude.

Third, for all of you who have made direct contributions of tribute, comments, quotes, or my quoting your existing written work, we are building a better world, one loving relationship at a time. Thank you, Alicia White, Altoria Houney, Amy Crystal Norse, Annemarie Van Rooyen, Chiquita Mullins – Lee, Daniela Babun, Donna Valentine, Freedom Pearson, Kirsty Downing, Lorraine Kolmacic Carey, Maria Schenck, Sheryl Owens and Tialila Kikon; my heart to your heart.

Fourth, I wish to thank the very special soul that helped me clearly see and understand my mission. "Hannelore Stumpf, we will always have Tokyo."

TRIBUTES

Love is multidimensional. It is a multitude of things. How can we really describe it in words when it runs through us like lightning through our veins? It is the magic. It is the beauty. It is the light. It is the rawness. It is the purpose. It is the direction. It is the passion. It is the thunder. It is our wild. It is the smell of grass in summer and the salt in the breeze by the sea. It is everything yet nothing we could ever completely know.

Amy Crystal Norse
Author of How I Found My Wild

Oscar Crawford is a scientist of Love! His scientific method involves humanity's, women and men's, capacity to live out their authentic selves through the love vehicles of spirit, soul, and body. Let's Talk About Love is the revelation through which readers experience the authentic depths of love.

Ani Vec Flewellen
a Practitioner of Toltec Wisdom

Oscar is a true lover of the world. He senses those that are in need of his love and understanding. He attracts those with ease. Truly blessed with a heightened gift, he gives himself to others when present with them.

Alicia White
Author of the Roar Trilogy

Oscar has a heart full of grace-filled with love. He is a generous soul always ready to share much love and appreciation. This world could be a better place with more people like him. I feel blessed to have cross paths with his beautiful soul.

Tialila Kikon
Poet and Author of Paper Cranes

"Oscar "gets it". He understands that it's not about the love you aren't **getting**; it's about the love you aren't **giving** that makes all the difference in your life on every level. O knows how to love and teaches it gracefully. I believe that you learn what you teach and we are all teaching something. O teaches love, and he grows in love every day. Not conditional love like you might see from a Hollywood film, but Conditionless Love, which isn't taught in our society."

Donna Valentine

Author, Composer, Musician, and Vocalist

Love has been a subject of search and rescue since the beginning of time. Ancient philosophers discussed about it. Social scientists study it. Theologians dance around it. Psychologists dissect it. We are still at a loss as to what love is.

Oscar Crawford has taken on the daunting task of taking us on a journey of discovery. He has spent years questioning, probing, and capturing the human experience associated with the pursuit and understanding of love.

Sheryl Owens

Retired Librarian Columbus, Ohio

I met Oscar Crawford some years ago on Facebook. We were authors and connected with the hopes of sharing interests and doing some cross promoting. I had read his books and come to find him an accomplished writer. More than that, I found him also a spiritual soul. It is evident in his words.

I have observed Oscar grow in his literary career and his media network. He helps others promote their works. He is a true Ambassador for Love's Sake.

He featured my co-author and me on his radio show. He helped promote my books. Most of all, he has been a true friend on whom I can rely to be there for moral support. He is always willing to have an open ear for me. I have confided in this man with several of my personal issues and he has always been there to listen, not judge but guide me, and gives me hope and unconditional love.

We have not met yet in person but when we do, I know it will seem like we have known each other from childhood. He has that ability to connect with your soul. If you are lucky enough to meet him in person or online, he will definitely leave an impact on you in a good way.

Oscar Crawford is truly a gifted light worker. I have seen him in action. I can attest to the help he has given others and myself. These types of souls are rare in this world. I treasure our friendship and am so proud of his mission to seek out what love really is.

Lorraine Kolmacic Carey
Author and Educator

Oscar Crawford is one of the most amazing people I have ever encountered. His writings demonstrate his character and give insight into him as a person. If you read carefully, you can see that he gets deep into real-world issues that affect many people.

Oscar shows passion, compassion, understanding, empathy, intelligence, caring, giving, loyalty and most of all He EXUDES LOVE in every sense of the word. Through his writings, we find enlightenment because he cares to learn and know about people "truths and walks of life". He clarifies that although we all bleed the same, we do not all love, care, express ourselves, and accept or tolerate things the same way. He declares that ok because we all arrive uniquely created.

He gets it! HE GETS PEOPLE. That is a breath of fresh air! I feel much honored to have been able to speak and communicate with such a loving and inspiring soul.

Maria Schenck
Actor and Airline Professional

Oscar is a beacon of hope for me, my lighthouse providing a comforting, guiding light to safety and home. Oscar's love breaks through the boundaries which society dictates and he selflessly holds out his hand to help those up who have stumbled along life's bumpy road. Love is the air to his lungs and the beat to his heart and he has taught me that the word 'family' also means 'unbreakable bond' and we can all live together harmoniously if we want to. Oscar is a key part of my family now and he has shown many others and me that love is what truly makes the world go round. Thank you my dear O for always being on my side, for believing in me, and for reaching out to me for no other reason than to share your love.

Kirsty Downing
Early Childhood Education Professional

We sometimes miss very important life lessons while focusing on irrelevant energies that keep us from our true and authentic selves. This can cause us to fall victim to energies and situations that possess no benefit for anyone. These are breaking points.

Then, you meet an Angel sent to you with a direct message from God. Their delivery is so gentle, it penetrates the walls we built and our walls fall down. We are now open to the energetic force that will push us into our divine path of purpose. This is what happened when I met Oscar Crawford, my Oh so awesome O.

Oscar is a Warrior for Love. His ability to see through physical transforming energy is amazing, thus my O so awesome O. Love looks different and boundaries disappear. When we recognize love, we see ourselves so much clearer than before. Thanks, Oscar for being a perfect mirror of divine reflection.

Freedom Pearson

Freedom of You
Love Anyhow Right Now
Choosing to Do it in and on Purpose

Love is the hope of every human. As we encounter people throughout life's journey, we hope to experience love and all its beneficence. Should you meet and engage Oscar Crawford, you will experience a glimpse of what love is.

Oscar believes in the power of love and exudes it wherever he goes. He has a heart for people and loves to listen to their stories to encourage them, counsel when necessary but most importantly to show them there is at least one human being that loves them and that would be him. To encounter Oscar is to know that love exists without judgment. You cannot meet Oscar without experiencing the joy of feeling loved.

Altoria Houney

Spiritual Emissary and Vocalist

THE PREFACE

Let's Talk About Love – a Guide to Love and Come Alive for the Awakening Mid- 30's Woman Living with PTSD resulting from Sexual Violence while a child is a book that has been brewing and writing itself inside me, my personal and my professional experience for more than thirty years. Love preoccupies my thinking. It has done so since I was a child and continues to preoccupy my thoughts and behavior as an aging adult.

As a loving soul, a human being, and a verstehen social scientist, one that has an empathic understanding of human behavior, I want to know what love is. I want to know what love is not. I want to know how more people can experience more love in their lives. I want to know how love can raise the quality of life in the lives of people across the Earth. I want to know how love can minimize and eliminate the potential for violence. I want to know.

I have known the time would come to share what I have learned of love throughout my travels and experience. From Asia to Eastern Europe, Canada to the West Indies, New York to Alaska, California to Florida and many other points across North America, I have met thousands of women and men of all ages, stages, colors, cultures, races, classes, and religions. They have shared their stories and experiences of love with me. They have informed me; inspired me, entertained me, and created memories within me that will last for all of my life.

I live with extreme gratitude for the privilege and gift of my experience with so many people across the Earth. If I had not lived my own amazing adventure and continue to live this incredible journey, I might not believe it even possible. My life experiences range from moments of traumatic injury, pain, and PTSD post–traumatic stress disorder to ecstatic moments of pure pleasure and joy with multiples more of the ecstatic.

I discover, experience, and share love wherever my life and love take me. Whether I am in the air, I am on the Earth, or I am beneath the Earth, the creative source prepares and provides experiences of love for me that are moments in ecstasy. Wherever I am, whenever I am, love's presence precedes arrival and waits for me like a loved one waiting for me at the airport, the train station, or bus station.

I am clear that my experience and personal story are inadequate to possess and articulate a complete knowledge of what love really is. Prior to the coming of 2018, I launched an investigation to explore with many across the Earth to explore what love is and what love is not. I want to know.

Is it possible to know what love is? We, humans, say, "YES!" What we really mean is that we really hope that we can fully experience love even when we acknowledged we do not fully know what love is.

We want it or believe we do. We want love. We want to love a special other and experience the love of a special other towards us. We hope for and believe in the magic of love. Whether we actually know what we are doing or not is an entirely different matter?

Is there such a thing as getting it right in love? Can we uncover ways to measure success in love?

For the investigation, I acknowledged the need to use existing technologies to gather and collect the thoughts of as many people as I could reach in my local and global orbit. To that end, I interviewed friends and family. I interviewed people while walking the streets of Metropolitan Phoenix, Arizona.

I talked to people on the bus, train, and plane. I reached out to the world through social media personally connecting to as many people in different nations as possible. I hosted radio broadcasts, blogs and news magazines seeking information.

British – American Rock Band Foreigner sang in 1984, "I Want to Know What Love Is." Further, they said, "I want YOU to show me." Who is or who are the YOU they referenced?

People across the Earth could feel the message in the song. It declared the common feeling of longing that rings and resonates in our hearts. People all over the Earth declare the same thing. We want to know what love is. We want YOU to show us.

Many of us feel we need another to show us the way. Who will show us the way? Who will show us how?

Humans everywhere desire to live the experience of love. The high hope is to live the experience of love with another that feels about us the same way we feel about them. That is the dream. We seek the hoped for joy of love. We want to love and experience and enjoy the love of that one special other that loves us.

Whatever love is, it preoccupies our species. We desperately want it because we believe love holds the answers that resolve the challenging human questions. We believe love will bring meaning to our lives in ways that nothing else can. We believe that love redeems our suffering whatever our experiences of suffering are or have been.

What common understandings across Planet Earth do we share about love? How do we understand

and approach love differently? What do we hope love will accomplish for us? Does code appear in our DNA matrix that programs and predisposes us to quest for love? What is love's purpose?

My heart burns, as do many of yours to know what love is. Does love possess a look that it might be recognized? Does love have a sound or a smell? Does love bring a feeling we can immediately recognize?

Let's Talk About Love – a Guide to Love and Come Alive for the Awakening Mid- 30's Woman Living with PTSD resulting from Sexual Violence while a child provides an approach to understanding love, knowing what love is, and knowing what love is not. Do you believe love is the key to realizing human dreams to achieve the perception of wholeness as much as is possible? Unbelievably, I actually do. I am all in.

The target of *Let's Talk About Love – a Guide to Love and Come Alive for the Awakening Mid- 30's Woman Living with PTSD resulting from Sexual Violence while a child* is the mid – 30's woman that experienced tragedies of domestic and sexual violence from her youth and adolescence at the hands of primarily male abusers. My high hope is that this book will accomplish the following:

It will speak directly to the heart of the mid – 30's woman living out the effects of decades of the

emotional and physical pain of post–traumatic
stress disorder.

It will inspire the healing of the mid – 30's
woman's emotional and physical pain.

It will help the affected many awaken to prepare for
lives of fulfilling love.

If you respond, "Yes, but how," I invite you to
turn the page. Let's Talk About Love begins now.

THE INTRODUCTION

I am the person that women have been telling their personal stories since I came home from the military in the early 1970's. I was 21 years old and entering Kentucky State University.

The Commonwealth of Kentucky created Kentucky State in 1879 as a Normal School. It provided colored students that could not attend The Commonwealth's segregated colleges and universities an opportunity for teacher education. This is the traditional school where my elders and ancestors had been educated and trained as teachers for Kentucky's Colored Schools beginning in the 1940's.

I was unclear about the "WHY" I had been chosen to be a preferred listener. All I knew was that I was listening to many stories women and younger girls needed to tell someone. I wondered if it happened because I was older. Most students in their senior year were 20 with 21 on the horizon. I did also consider a spiritual mission might be hovering over me or forming I had not yet become aware.

I found myself listening to the stories of being late, being pregnant, or choosing to engage the action of terminal fetal arrested development. I was there to hear their love stories going wrong. I was there for the questions about often choosing Mr. Wrong while seeking out and hoping for Mr. Right.

I had no answers for these perplexing experiences and the questions that followed. I never pretended I did. What I did seem to have was an abundant ability to be present to listen and offer care without judgment.

After completing university in 1978, I served the African Methodist Episcopal Church and other non – profit corporations that served people and community interests. The stories that followed exponentially grew in dimension among adult women. Now I was dealing with unhappy wives of cheating and abusive husbands.

I had married in 1977, the year before I graduated university in 1978. Three daughters arrived over the next four years. As my own story evolves, it is clear my marriage will not lead to happily ever after.

My three daughters were the only beauty resulting from marriage to my children's mother. I love being a father. When it was over, I had my three daughters and I was happy. We lived a joy-filled life. We all went to school during the week. We travelled on the weekend at the expense of groups hiring me to speak and teach. We stayed in some exciting hotels and resorts. My girls though their dad was the man.

I would be the only dad at Brownie Scout meetings after I became single. I am hearing more women's stories. It was complicated but I would not trade being who I am for all the convenience in the world. I was not interested in coupling up with anyone even if but for a moment. I did not welcome adding anyone else's drama to my life at that time. I am living out an undefined spiritual mission into my adult life.

In the mid - 1980's, women I met socially and professionally began to reveal to me that their fathers, brothers, and others used them for sex while children. Nothing in undergraduate school or graduate school prepared me for this. The stories came and I asked, "Why me?"

It happened so often, it troubled me. I needed to understand how I was attracting the women telling me their stories. There was only one person that I knew that could help me sort this out, Hannelore Stumpf. I boarded a plane in Columbus, Ohio and flew 2,000 miles to Phoenix, Arizona to consult with her. We had met years earlier in Japan.

When we talked, I told her the stories women were telling me. I told her I needed to understand why what had happened to women as children affected their lives into their mid – 30's and beyond. More than that, I told her that I needed to understand how I was attracting women telling me these stories.

Beyond the mystery of the "WHY" I learn what I must learn, I am aware I have a heart for the hurting but I am as lost as two left shoes for what to do and how to help. I have no clue for what to do other than be present, caring, and without judgment. I possess no skill set to minister help and direction in this case. I possess the desire to help people in pain to heal. To do so, I must acquire useful information to develop a plan.

My friend and mentor laughed at me and said, "Silly man, do you remember all I shared as I cried in your presence when we met in Tokyo that first evening?"

I acknowledged I did with the nod of my head. We had been part of a team in Japan and Korea to examine the distinctions between the spirituality of the Korean People and the Japanese People.

I had heard of a woman on the team that had three earned doctoral degrees. I wanted to meet her. I tried to explain my interest to the hotel desk clerk. After listening, he pointed in the direction of the escalator and said, "I believe the lady of whom you speak goes there just now."

When I turned, I saw a woman classically dressed floating up the escalator like an angel. I lost my breath for a moment. She was stunning. She looked as if she could have stepped directly off the set of the antebellum academy award winning film, Gone with the Wind.

She was dressed in a pink ensemble. I remember the moment as if it just happened. Her dress was pink tapered to her waist with large ruffles on the bottom and light ruffles on top. With shoes and bag to match, her hat was the crowning glory of the ensemble. It was a large pink hat with ruffles fit for the celebrations of Kentucky Derby.

I pursued her up the escalator, introduced myself, and asked if we might have coffee. She gave me the once over as if reading me and said yes. We agreed to meet that evening.

I learned she was a clinical psychologist. As we sat together, she told me she was recently out a 20 plus year marriage. She had been married to a medical doctor that had become a violent and abusive alcoholic. He had been abusive to her for a number of years. She held on to hope that he would change. When her awakening to self - love moment came, she found the courage to walk away.

After reminding me of our beginning, she put on her clinical psychologist hat. She continued by telling me the women I was meeting had determined me, as she had earlier in Tokyo, to be a safe place and a safe person to share those things that they had never shared.

I followed with, "I do not know what to do." She simply said to me, "Be patient. You will."

I do not know how but this took the heavy off. I now know why women select me to tell their experiences. I am no longer troubled. My mission is clear. We hug and declare our continuing love and friendship. It is time to get back to Sky Harbor International Airport and on my way home through Port Columbus International Airport.

Not long after my time with friend and mentor, I met with a professional woman about a training event I would facilitate at the Central Ohio University she served. We are having dinner to go over the final details of the activity.

When dinner is over and our business concluded, I prepare to stand. I will shake her hand, pay the check, and depart. As I, back my chair up to stand, she tugs at my cloud blue cuff-linked shirtsleeve and asks if she can tell me one more thing. She has tears in her eyes. I have no idea what I am about to hear but I offer to her my handkerchief.

A set of emotions resulting from her being sexually abused, raped as a little girl poured out of her. It had plagued her for more than 30 years. Today, her liberation moment had come. I listen to how the effects of post - traumatic stress disorder had affected her life and development.

She concluded with she knew I was the person she knew she could tell. She knew I would be present and focused while she shared. She knew I would listen with a caring heart. She knew I would offer no judgment.

My heart broke for her. We had known each other for years and worked together many times. This moment pushed my poker playing skills to its limit.

I do consider myself a competent poker player. Being a poker player taught me to maintain a straight face. Whatever cards I hold or whatever I hear, my face reveals no emotion. That was a huge asset.

Our moment ended with a hug and a woman walking away with a huge weight lifted from her emotional life. She had a smile on her face that beamed. I saw it as she looked back at me once as she walked away.

I now possessed the beginning of a response. Simply be present. Listen with a caring heart. Offer no judgment. Be as affirming as possible offering opportunity for the hurting person to feel good about their accomplishment. They have shared what happened.

These events set in motion the clarity of my mission to this day. The mission is simple. Help the hurting heal. Help them prepare to live a life of fulfilling love beginning with self - love.

CHAPTER ONE – THE MISSION

The conscious energy of love has been, is now, and forever will be the only power able to shift the heart of humanity from aggression to mutual, harmonious, and peaceful coexistence. When we no longer wish to bring harm to ourselves, we will cease to bring harm to others. ~Magi Aata

The Mission of *Let's Talk About Love – a Guide to Love and Come Alive for the Awakening Mid- 30's Woman Living with PTSD resulting from Sexual Violence while a child* is to collect and establish core information of what love is and what love is not leading to the development of a Guide to Love and Come Alive. People everywhere on Earth, WE, want to love and experience love in our lives. We prepare for love to the best of our understanding and ability. We seek love because we believe love is the best answer and only approach to usher in an era of joy with the potential to end all human conflict.

We have so much to say about our thoughts of love without a single, simple, and practical definition of what love is. Can it be that love is simply acting out the desire to be present, caring, and without judgment as we share ourselves intimately with a significant other or special others? Can it be that simple?

Some of us have concluded that love is a feeling. We do not know where the feeling comes from or where it goes. We just want it.

We collect information from every experience and every thought of love but capturing love to possess it feels just beyond our grasp. Is it possible that love itself does the choosing for where and within whom it will locate and when?

This obstacle to knowing what love is, definitively, does not prevent people across the Earth continuing to have much to say about what we do not know. Our high hope is that information gathered for Let's Talk About Love may prove to be beneficial to our developing a clearer understanding of what love is and what love is not.

This quest has led to one substantial conclusion to which there appears to be little to no evidence to the contrary. Love is not a thing. Love is an intangible and invisible energy. When love shows up in the lives and behavior of women and men, it often arrives unannounced.

There exist few indicators of where love lives constantly beyond the lives and hearts of human mothers. While there may be some limited exceptions, a mother's love stands the most real and profound presence and expression of love on Planet Earth.

Most mothers will love their children unconditionally, no matter what. Exceptions to this rule exist too, but they are not the norm. Our mothers open all of themselves to bring us into the world and their arms generally remain open to their children and their children's children all of their lives.

People crave love without a clear understanding of what love is. What we have settled on is that love is a worthy idea and we dedicate ourselves to its pursuit as the moth focused only on reaching the bright hot white light.

We cannot simply go looking for love. There exist no tools for the search. Neither radar nor sonar can detect love.

Love's experience is not the result of an achievement. One cannot look for love with success. One may only prepare for love by first becoming love. We, all of us and each of us, must first become the love we have the desire to experience and share with another or others before we are prepared for love.

To this end, love is like the wind. We cannot see the wind to say here it is. We are limited to observation of where the wind has been and what the wind has done.

If we see a windmill turn, we observe what the wind had done and may continue to do. We can observe the result of powerful windstorms, tornados, typhoons, and hurricanes. All these tend to leave behind the evidence of destruction of where the wind has been.

We may describe love much the same way. We cannot see love. We do not know where love is. We can only observe evidence of where love has been through what love has done or is doing.

Acts of love demonstrating the highest level of care for refugees of catastrophic events arrive in the form of food, water, clothes and health care. Acts of love can come in the form of gifts of care from one person to another or groups to other groups.

All who seek love are compelled to ask how civilized and spiritual people war with each other over ideas of power, politics, economics, and religion. We ask ourselves, how a civilized and spiritual people can allow for the sexploitation of women and children to satisfy the perverse desires of people that will pay to use them and then dispose of them. We ask ourselves, why a civilized and spiritual people allow for one-half of the world's population to live in poverty. Where is the love?

To date, we ask ourselves, why love; our highest

value has not made a significant difference in these
conditions. It is simply because we do not possess
sufficient preparation for love as individuals, families,
communities, and nations.

What makes love so important that people will
give their bodies and sell their souls hoping to get it?
What makes love so important that people will give all
their money hoping to get it? What makes love so
important that people will sacrifice their health and
life to get it or experience it even if but for a singular
moment?

What makes love so important that people will
travel the world looking for love hoping to get it?
What makes love so important that people will lie,
cheat, steal, and kill hoping to get it? What makes love
so important that people will commit utterly stupid
acts hoping to get it? It is because love is not
something to get. Love is something to become and
be.

A high school teacher runs away with an
underage student because she is in love with the
student. When found by law enforcement, the judicial
system charges the teacher with kidnapping,
unlawfully taking a minor across state lines beyond
their home state, sexual misconduct with a minor, and

statutory rape. Convictions can lead to concurrent sentencing for a minimum of 15 to 25 years. They can result in the consecutive sentencing of 50 years or more.

Writers, poets, and artists have portrayed love as a form of madness for which humans lose all sense of reason and logic. What causes a man and a woman that cannot speak the same language on opposing sides of a war to experience love for each other in the hostile environment of war?

What causes a spiritual leader to give up her or his years of community and family service and influence for the affection of a commercial sex worker leaving their followers stunned? Their report to the question of why is simple. He or she did it for their perception of a moment's love they could not find anywhere else.

What causes a Monarch to abdicate, relinquish, or give up the throne for a commoner? Why does this final royal act for one, not the Monarch's equal stun the people of the kingdom? The former monarch's answer to the question of why is simple. The monarch did it for love.

What causes presidents, members of Congress, governors, other government officials, corporate and community leaders to risk their lifelong reputations for sexual affairs? What causes husbands and wives to cheat on each other?

Why do the powerful prey on the powerless to take what they want? All engage these behaviors for the feel-good of temporarily having what they want and some call that love.

The reality here is there is no existing trustworthy DIY do it yourself guide to love. We can observe courtship rituals or read how-to books of 10 steps to Your Dream Love but not be able to make them work.

Because we do not know how to love ourselves properly, we resort to how we dress, how we smell, how much money we have to buy things to attract people we hope will like us. Many will as long as the money and things hold out.

We use money and other material things hoping they can do for us what we do not know how to do. We are devastated when the relationships developed following these approaches end in emotional devastation.

Whatever love is, we are not there yet. Love is an invisible and intangible energy, force, and power. We can neither see love nor touch love. Love can arrive like a gentle breeze or like a hurricane. When would now be a good time for you to prepare for love to become the love you want to share with another or others?

What does all this have to do with beginning the healing of traumas previously experienced by the mid – 30's woman? I am so thankful you are asking this question. All things become clear.

Take a moment now to examine whether or not Chapter 1 has been of benefit to you and your understanding of love. Examine your personal thoughts by stepping inside the following questions and your own experience. Your truth will reveal itself.

Moments for Personal Thought

What are my personal notions of love? How did I learn them? Are they working for me? Are they working for the people in my life?

_____

_____

_____

_____

What did Chapter 1 inform me love is? What did it inform me love is not?

_____

_____

_____

_____

What is the craziest thing or the riskiest behavior I have done for love? Did it work? How did I feel about myself afterwards? What did I learn?

_____

_____

_____

_____

What has Chapter 1 suggested to me that will help me establish a practical understanding of what love is?

_____

_____

_____

_____

What are my conclusions of love after reading Chapter 1?

_____

_____

_____

What must I immediately stop doing after reading
Chapter 1?

_____

_____

_____

What must I immediately begin to do after reading
Chapter 1?

_____

_____

_____

What is my Love Mission? My Love Mission is

_____

_____

Chapter Two
The Troublesome Gods

One of the primary human dreams is to magically meet and fall passionately in love with the one person that the very thought of them prompts our soul to reach the chaos of critical mass, explode, and become a lasting and empowering peace. The perception of this hoped-for experience is that it will complete us so that we want nothing more than to sustain the experience of joy for a lifetime.

This on rare occasions happens but this rare occurrence is the exception and not the rule. It is an immature perspective of love's task in human life. It is an immature approach to hope love will magically happen. The challenge is we humans live to believe in magic.

How did we arrive at such a mythic fairytale notion? It arrived because of stories that are written to help us mortals make sense out of what cannot be understood, the gods' dominion over humans and human's affairs.

This dilemma comes to us from the story of the Greek Gods of Olympus as described by Aristophanes in Plato's work, the Symposium. The Gods believed the human *Originals (my classification)* the two - faced, four - handed, and four - legged humans to be monstrosities, albeit clever monstrosities. The Gods feared the humans could represent a challenge to their dominion.

Zeus, the King of the Gods acted. He cut the humans in half and ordered his son Apollo to have the halves see their wounds to maintain control over them. Zeus threatened to cut them in half again if they did not conform to the demanded order.

The half humans then became preoccupied with themselves and their pitiful condition. This is one origin story of the idea to divide and conquer. Human history is replete with its exercise. Half humans continued to live out lives of misery, suffering, and confusion drifting lost and alone without hope of reunion to wholeness.

Eventually, Zeus had pity on the half humans. He decided to place the genitals of each part to face their front of them so they might take comfort in joining each other to soothe their sorrows. We have been working on soothing our sorrows since.

This myth is not so different from the Torah's version of creation where it is necessary for the two-part creation of human beings, female and male, to join to become one flesh Genesis 2 vss 21 - 25. This joining represented a form of wholeness unable to be experienced functioning as a single entity.

We, humans, are dedicated to this quest to return to wholeness. It is our quest to love. We seek the experience of love, as we understand love to give our lives relevance and meaning. We find this condition of incompleteness and being alone intolerable.

COMPLICATIONS

Complications or the things that get in the way of our getting what we want are simply opportunities to learn. People can be very slow arriving at this awareness.

We, humans, complicate our lives because we have not evolved to dictate the terms of our lives on our own terms for ourselves. Some of us are addicted and dependent upon the ideas of another or others to do our thinking and provision for us, often without considering or realizing the costs for doing so. From the moment we become conscious of our awareness, most of us accept the necessity to conform to the ideas of others, convention, and tradition. Doing so sacrifices the most amazing gift we did not give ourselves, those of our lives, and our consciousness.

Our first thought programmers are our parents and our immediate family. They simply believe what they are doing to be right and in our best interests. It can be but more often than not, it is not. Their influence can more often than not prove to be the crippling of potential to discovery and personal achievement.

How does this affect the mid – 30's woman. How many women in their mid – 30's must live with the horrors of their fathers, brothers, or others using them for sex as children? Too scared to tell anyone for fear of further harm, these emotionally hurting women never told anyone what happened. They live unaware of the effects of these experiences on their lives as their lives evolve.

The mid – 30's woman that has survived this experience of rape and incest may not be aware of her arrested development. This resulted from her emotional development halting when her traumatic events began. Although her emotional development ended, her chronological and biological development did not.

Arrested Psychological Development is being 'stuck' in an emotional level of development. Depending on the timing of trauma (childhood, adolescent, or teen) determines the symptoms of Arrested Psychological Development.

The mid – 30's woman grew older. Without the intervention of therapy, she remains in the emotional context of the age when her abuse began. If she was five, even as an adult she functions emotionally as a five-year-old.

The influence of our social network of peers in school comes next. We want to fit in to earn their acceptance, their approval, and have them like us.

The third in this medium for social human control is religion. Religion's objective asserts a moral force on the behavior of practitioners to be good or God will be angry and severely punish. This hoodoo continues to enslave many. There are exceptions to this personal conclusion.

James Redfield's classic work, the Celestine Prophecy taught us the consequences of leaving others to the direction of our spiritual lives, *the expressed personal gratitude and appreciation for our life, consciousness, and directed intention.* In his work, he shared what happened when Roman Catholic women and men grew disenchanted with the church because they became aware of the corrupt and immoral behavior of priests. The more things change, the more things remain the same. Celibacy may be a vocational choice but denying the need for sexual expression is not.

Too many adult children now bear witness to the cruel and criminal sexual expression of celibacy. Priests raping children are not celibate. They are criminal.

Redfield reported that when people left the church, they went out in search of meaning. Incidentally, this was the beginning of the exploration of the world. When the explorers went out, they did not find meaning. When they returned without finding meaning, they had returned with something else. They had plundered the material possessions and taken lands from indigenous peoples.

Taking from the savages (so-called) discovered in the lands found in the New World had proven profitable. This was the beginning of the colonial expansion of Europeans and the taking of lands occupied by indigenous others on the continents of North America, South America, India, and Africa.

Centuries later after raping the lands and the people, the conquerors returned after surrendering the lands to the indigenous peoples because they were no longer profitable. Redfield concludes this gives rise to a coming critical mass of spiritual energy to people across the Earth to love each other in ways that yield cooperation and peace for the sake of survival. It is about time.

The gods of the contemporary world, power and greed, are hardly different from the gods of Olympus. Both want to control the human destiny for their own interests and benefit. The influence of the human reality of the western world directs that we secure ways to distinguish ourselves and establish our relevance in ways that we can achieve sustainable commercial value and profit.

The fourth tier in the medium of control is the entity of mass media. This includes the high-powered Internet resting comfortably in our hands concealed in our 21st Century phones. Driven by profit, mass media informs us we should all look like film stars and other celebrity high profile personalities.

We are influenced to eat what they eat, dress as they dress, and simply do everything as they do it. This design influences us and convinces us that we will immediately elevate our self – perception and make ourselves feel good when we do.

A healthy self - perspective is a good thing only when it is self – developed and not because of the programming of external influences. When my children were growing up and wanted things other children had, I explained to them why as their father, I would not invest in those kinds of things for them.

I needed them to discover there is limited to no

value in being just like everybody else. They would have to earn the money to do those things themselves. I assured them if they wanted things or experiences that would help them realize themselves and their own personal interests, I would break the bank to help them make it happen.

The final tier in the medium for control is ultimately the most dangerous evil of all, our untrained and unrestrained minds. Our minds are ours. We must train them to serve our interests and the interests of all we might benefit from ourselves to our families and beyond to others.

We have no right to control others or their minds. They do not belong to us. Others have no right to control our minds or us. We do not belong to them.

Our minds are the gifts that came with the privilege of our birth from the creative source. With our minds, we make the critical choices for how we will live and what we will create with our life.

This is the beginning of love. Until we awaken to this love, we will wander aimlessly in the dark hoping to touch something or someone that makes us feel good for a moment. That discovery is our individual privilege and responsibility to define for ourselves whether it conforms to what songwriter, author, musician, idealist, and quantum enthusiast

Donna Valentine calls the Conscious Masses Mindset. Donna chooses to live the Way of the Heart.

What love is, that is yet to come. For now, what love is not reveals itself in the history of our species. Hang on! We are going somewhere.

Take a moment now to examine whether or not Chapter 2 has been of benefit to you and your developing understanding of love. Examine your personal thought by stepping inside the following questions and your own experience. Your truth will reveal itself.

Moments for Personal Thought

Are my personal notions of love fixed or fluid? Am I learning new perspectives? Will what I am learning serve love? Do I observe what I am learning work for others in my life?

_____

_____

_____

_____

Will I continue to do crazy things or risky behavior for love? Why would I make this choice? Why do I think this behavior will work better now than before? How will I feel if it still does not work? Will I look at everything from now on as a learning experience to gather new information?

_____

_____

_____

_____

What has Chapter 2 suggested to me that will help me establish or enhance a more practical understanding of what love is? Have I further learned what love is not? If I have learned more what love is not, what did I learn?

_____

_____

_____

What are my conclusions of love after reading Chapter 2?

_____

_____

_____

_____

What must I immediately stop doing because of reading Chapter 2?

_____

_____

_____

_____

What must I immediately begin to do after reading Chapter 2?

_____

_____

_____

Has the sense of my Love Mission changed since reading Chapter 2 or does my sense of my Love Mission remain the same?

What is my Love Mission? If it remains the same, I reiterate it to reinforce it to myself. The more I affirm my mission to myself, the more it becomes a real force in my life.

My Love Mission is

_____

_____

_____

Chapter Three – The Profile

The profile of the mid – 30's woman awakening to self - love is that she has been one bouncing from sullen to angry to depressed . From her arrested development, the place in time her emotional development stopped, she believed nobody cared about her. Nobody protected her from harm. Her emotional responses to life have developed to provide her a form of self – protection.

This makes almost anyone resembling her attacker from years ago or any man subject to her hostile response she could not give to protect herself when raped as a child. She does not know why she responds this way but thinks of herself as a no-nonsense woman. She may be guilty of taking out a lifetime's anger on whoever is in front of her from moment to moment until someone cares about her enough to risk intervening and calling her attention to her behavior.

She is primarily single but can be married. She has two children or more from the two or more long-term relationships that have lasted from 18 months to three to five years. These may or may not have been marriages.

She has completed post–secondary education

through community colleges and universities. She works hard but her hardest task is getting along with others as she always feels she is under attack and must protect her interests. She had a mother that did not protect her. Because of that, she has difficulty with male and female supervisors.

She has issues with her weight since a child. She kept on extra weight to be less appealing. She considered appearing less attractive would make her safer. This is not a fixed absolute, simply an identified trend from interviews.

She discovered her choices in boyfriends early on and lovers later came with a propensity for dominance and violence. She asked herself repeatedly how she managed to attract the same personality.

Unable to represent her interests or even know exactly what her interests are, she initially submits to her latest lover and the demands of his stronger personality until she could no longer tolerate them and their mean spirited behavior towards her. In context, her personal behavior is self – destructive choosing love interests that consistently hurt her.

In Reece and Brandt's 1987 third Edition of Effective Human Relations in Organizations, Richard Grote of Dallas Performance Systems says, "People treat us with the respect that we place on ourselves."

The mid – 30's woman yet to awaken to self – love has not yet discovered this principle. All that has consistently happened to her at the hands of others and behaviors of others affirm her sense of being a person of little to no value.

She has been the victim of sexual violence before 12 years old and as young as 5 years old. She has been the victim of the brutality of domestic violence by age 15. This can come from the hands of the same man, her father.

This profile is general and limited to the observations of the writer over 30 years of experience with affected women. Exceptions exist. The awakening soul of women to self – love can occur at any age and stage and her healing begin. The delay in her healing happens when no therapeutic treatment response follows her experiences of sexual violence. While the healing can begin at any age and stage, the propensity of the women I have met and worked with is in her mid – 30's.

Seven in 10 mid–30's women I have met the past three decades shared with me that members of their family or friends of their family used them for sex before age 12. These traumatic events result in feelings of shame that go undisclosed until their mid – 30's.

They have told no one for two reasons. The first results from the feeling of extreme shame. The second results from concluding no one would believe their story.

Since the mid-1980's, I have consistently heard this report from hundreds of women across the world. This behavior happens across all cultures, religions, ages, and socioeconomic levels. The urban woman is as affected as the rural woman is. While it happens in all cultures, Indigenous Women in the United States experience the highest rates of sexual violence of all women. 94% of Native American Women say they have been raped or coerced into sex, 94%.

The Post – Traumatic Stress resulting from these experiences of rape linger in women for decades. Mid – 30's women begin to explore whether what happened to them as children affects their mental health, career, and relationships. The effects of sexual trauma untreated for more than two decades can cause bouts of anger and depression, eating disorders, panic attack, substance abuse, and other dysfunctional behaviors without an awareness of why.

Somewhere in the United States, a woman experiences rape every two minutes. This calculation results from 720 cases of rape per day in the U.S. from reported cases and guestimates based on formulas created by organizations presenting them. Of women who are raped in their lifetime: 17.9% are Caucasian, 11.9% are Latina, 18.8% are African-American, 34.1% are American Indian or Alaskan Native, and 6.8% are Asian or Pacific Islander 24.4% are mixed race according to the **Connecticut Alliance to End Sexual Violence.** The Alliance reports this finding in Women of Color and Sexual Assault – Racism and Sexual Assault.

If two women experience rape in the United States every two minutes that is 720 women every day, that equals more than a quarter of a million women each year. That number is low and the reality could be as high as ten times that number. All the women that do not report their experience are the women who live out their arrested development without the intervention of treatment until their soul awakening to +self – love experience in their mid – 30's.

Take a moment now to examine whether or not Chapter 3 has been of benefit to you and your developing understanding of love. Examine your personal thought by stepping inside the following questions and your own experience. Your truth will reveal itself.

Moments for Personal Thought

Have I accepted my experience of rape as a child affects my relationships with others and myself? If I have, please list the ways I believe my relationships affected. Second, list the ways I believe I can make a difference in and improve my relationship with others and myself.

_____

_____

_____

_____

What did Chapter 3 suggest to me that love is for me? What did it suggest to me that love is not?

_____

_____

_____

_____

Did I feel protected by my family as a child and teen? Was I afraid of my family as a child or a teen?

_____

_____

_____

_____

How many of the items of the profile of the mid – 30's woman affected by the Post–Traumatic Disorder resulting from rape as a child or teen do I identify in myself? What has Chapter 3 suggested to me that will help me establish a more practical understanding of what of love is for me? What have I more clearly learned in Chapter 3 that love is not?

_____

_____

_____

_____

What are my conclusions of love after reading Chapter 3?

_____

_____

_____

_____

What must I immediately stop doing because of reading Chapter 3?

_____

_____

_____

_____

What must I immediately begin to do after reading Chapter 3?

_____

_____

_____

_____

Has my perception of my Love Mission changed? If yes, how has it changed? How will I engage my enhanced perception of my Love Mission?

_____

_____

Chapter Four – What Happened Had Nothing to Do with YOU

You cannot go back and rewrite your past. When you stand still at your past, it will always be against the expense of your future. ~Annemarie Van Rooyen

What happened to you had nothing to do with you. Whether your rapes happened when a little girl, a teen, or an adult; what happened to you had absolutely nothing to do with you. It had to do only with the uncontrolled and savage sexual rage of animal human males.

Perpetrators of these crimes against humanity caused you and other victims to suffer pain and anguish for years. Legal demands that they account for their sexually violent behavior does not happen enough. Out of 1,000 cases of rape, 310 cases reported to police. 57 of 310 reports lead to arrest. 11 of 57 cases got to prosecutors. 7 of the 11 cases that go to prosecutors lead to felony conviction. 6 rapists of the 7 conviction actually go to jail. Data comes from the RAINN, the Rape, Abuse, and Incest National Network

The events of these painful experiences remain largely hidden. Too often, these events do go unreported. The shame resulting from these experiences causes little girls to become teens that become adults not able to tell or reveal what happened to them. The Me Too Movement brings change that encourages women to come out of their darkness and isolation to bring their stories to the light.

In the meantime, the result of not sharing what happened becomes living in arrested development for decades into adulthood. Because they could tell, they could not receive help. The good news is that it is never too late to get help.

Socrates said at his trial for impiety and corrupting youth that the unexamined life is not worth living. He had choices to avoid the death penalty of drinking hemlock. All he had to do to live was accept exile from Athens, Greece or live a life of silence. He could not do either. He would die with his honor.

The moment the mid-30's woman awakens to self–love, she begins to examine her life and the traumatic experiences of her development as a child and a teen. Her consciousness begins to grow and expand.

When she awakens to self–love, it is a new concept to her. It is a bit frightening at first. She searches to understand how what happened to her as a child may have affected her life and behavior as an adult and how this has affected her perception of herself. Next, she must answer the question she asks, "What can I do to change?"

YES becomes the response to the litany of her soul-searching inquiry. She asks, "Is it possible my relationship with my own self – destructive behavior is a result of what happened to me as a child? Yes! Is it possible that I continue to attract violent and abusive men and women in my life because of what happened to me when I was a child? Yes!

"Is it possible that the reasons my personal and professional relationships do not work out results from what happened to me as a child? Yes! Is it possible that my poor parenting skills result from what happened to me as a child? Yes!

"Is it possible that I am often nervous and anxious something bad will happen to me because of what happened to me as child? Yes! Is it possible that my bouts of anger and depression result from what happened to me as a child? Yes! Yes! Yes!"

This mid–30's woman awakening to self–love now knows and understands why she fears when the lights go out at night and the house is quiet. That was when her daddy slipped into her room with his index finger to his lips saying, "Shhh baby."

When her father began to touch her, she cried saying, "Daddy, Please don't hurt me." This did not stop this devil ravaging the body of the little girl child that is his own daughter.

She remembers how she never wanted to be alone with her daddy or her brothers. She remembers held down, her mouth covered, and things happening to her she could not stop and she could not bring herself to tell. Intense shame followed along with the hiding of the experience.

A lifetime of memories floods through her like the mushrooming cloud of a nuclear explosion. This is her turning point. This is the moment she wants her future to be radically different from her past. If no one else will love her properly, she will begin to love herself properly. She does not forget the past but denies her past the privilege to hold her prisoner for another second. Righteous self – love begins.

This is the moment that she decides she will get help to process her experiences. Now, she will move on with her life with newfound purpose. She puts her emotional development back on course. Arrested Development is over. There is catching up to do and personal emotional growth to experience.

Some mothers blamed the daughters for enticing their husbands and brothers. It would not have happened if the girls had not asked for it. This is a common response even as the 21st Century Me Too Movement grows. Blame the traumatized victim not only for what happened to them but also for their experience of PTSD, Post – Traumatic Stress Disorder.

On March 12, 2013, Susan Babbel, Ph.D., M.F.T. (Marriage and Family Therapy) wrote for Psychology Today, an article entitled Trauma: Childhood Sexual Abuse and subtitled, Sexual abuse can lead to Post Traumatic Stress Disorder (PTSD). Dr. Babbel asserts these symptom outcomes of sexual abuse of children. They include:

Withdrawal or mistrust of adults

Potential to Suicide

Difficulty relating to others except in sexual or seductive ways

Unusual interest in or avoidance of all things sexual or physical

Sleep problems, nightmares, fears of going to bed

Frequent accidents or self-injurious behaviors

Refusal to go to school, or to the doctor, or home

Secretiveness or unusual aggressiveness

Sexual components to drawings and games

Neurotic reactions (obsessions, compulsiveness, phobias)
Habit disorders (biting, rocking)
Unusual sexual knowledge or behavior
Prostitution
Forcing sexual acts on other children
Extreme fear of being touched
Unwillingness to submit to a physical examination

Studies show children that experience sexual abuse tend to recover quicker and with better results if they have a supportive, caring adult, ideally a parent, consistently in their life, *provided there exists an awareness of the traumatic events in the child's life, legal remedy pursued as well as a treatment response for their care and recovery. (Italics are my own.)*

This criminal activity not only happens in civilian life but also in military life. When I first began to examine the data on sexual assault, I heard a report on NPR while driving that spoke of the sexual assault of women in the military. Women that had been victims of rape as children or teens before entering service likely would again while on active duty service.

The tragedy further expands when women experience the sexual assault of rape while serving in the theaters of war. Many of these women Soldiers and Marines did not receive their injuries from violent acts of the enemy. Theirs came by friendly fire when their brothers in arms acted out their savage testosterone and out of control sexual rage.

Jimmy Zuma writes in the Tucson Sentinel website that sexual assault of women in the military identified as friendly fire rape. An estimated 19,000 friendly fire rapes occur every year in the military. A military woman serving in Iraq is more likely to experience rape by a fellow soldier than be killed by enemy fire.

John Burnett reporting for NPR's All Things Considered posted an article entitled RAPE AND THE MILITARY and sub–titled MAJORITY OF SEXUAL ASSAULTS GO UNREPORTED IN ARMED SERVICES. He wrote that in June 1991, former National Guard Staff Sgt. Sharon Mixon was gang-raped by six soldiers. A military policeman said to her, "That's what you get for being a woman in a war zone." Mixon decided not to report the assault to her commander.

When former Army Pfc. Susan Upchurch told a female sergeant another soldier raped her, the sergeant directed her not to report the crime. Upchurch reported it anyway. Specialist Alexandro Jones' eventual conviction led to his sentence of 15 years.

One thing remains certain that love is not, love is not sexual harassment, sexual assault, sexual violence or friendly fire. Love is not all the polite words that mean the express savage brutality of rape.

Take a moment now to examine whether or not Chapter 4 has been of benefit to you and your developing understanding of love. Examine your personal thought by stepping inside the following questions and your own experience. Your truth will reveal itself.

Moments for Personal Thought

Am I clear that the rape of a child or teen that does not receive legal remedy for sexual criminal acts and/or follow-up treatment for care and recovery lives in emotional arrested development?

_____

_____

_____

How do you understand awakening to self – love? Do you have a personal practice of self - love?

_____

_____

_____

Has Chapter 4 enhanced your perspectives on what love is or what love is not? What is your conversation with yourself saying to you?

_____

_____

_____

What are my conclusions of love after reading Chapter 4? What must I immediately stop doing because of reading Chapter 4?

_____

_____

_____

_____

Has what you have learned inspired purpose of activity for your life after reading Chapter 4? What does love have to do with your inspired purpose?

_____

_____

_____

What must I immediately begin to do after reading Chapter 4?

_____

_____

_____

Has the sense of my love mission changed since reading Chapter 4 or does my sense of my love mission remain the same?

What is my Love Mission? If it remains the same, reiterate it to reinforce to yourself. The more you affirm your mission to yourself, the more it becomes a real force in your life.

My Love Mission is

_____

_____

Chapter Five
The Awakening to Love

Awakening that does not awaken the sleeper to love has roused her in vain. ~Jessamyn West

Recovery as a therapeutic process asserts to provide women and men with intervention strategies to end their self – destructive behavior. Recovery's high hope is that it will not only accomplish helping the addicted women and men stop doing what is killing them, their relationships, and their professional lives but will also help to restore their lives to functional responsibility. Recovery seeks to help people affected by addiction heal and reclaim their lives.

The mid – 30's woman awakening to self – love has no one to turn to but herself in the moment. Her awakening arrives when she accepts that she is tired of hurting. Her sole focus is now on her. She will take that first courageous look in the mirror knowing that she is not responsible for what happened to her.

She knows why other people do not seem to like her because she has spent a lifetime in emotional pain not liking who she has been. She vows while looking at the woman in the mirror that she is coming out of arrested development. She will help the little girl she was to heal and evolve to live a life of self – love responsibly loving herself first.

Recovery and restoration are not her goals. She focuses on her own personal development to build the life she wants to live. She accepts that none of us should receive praise or blame for the past. It is what it is. What we can do is intentionally develop ourselves through healing and customizing our environments and our relationships in ways that affirm us, liberate us, and empower us to become the best version of ourselves possible.

The Six Commitments of the Awakened to Love Mid – 30's Woman

This mid – 30's woman first commitment is one of gratitude for the power greater than her bringing her to the awakening to love and value herself. The second commitment is to her. She will do nothing and be involved with no one that is not in her or her family's best interest.

The third commitment is to take advantage of every available opportunity to continue her spiritual healing, her personal and professional development. Her fourth commitment is to reach out to as many women as possible to help them come to their own experience of awakening.

Her fifth commitment is to experience joy in her

life and it will come because of keeping the first four commitments. The sixth commitment is a commitment to love, to become and be the love she wants to share with another or others.

The Awakening

People awakened to love do not need prompts to show love to people, animals, or nature. Love is like breath to the awakened. It is their moral imperative. The awakened give love and show love with every opportunity. It is what the awakened do. Two types of the awakened to love exist.

Type 1

These are born awakened. They become the human angels amongst us. Their love is natural.

This esteemed few are they that are born with sensitive hearts and an insatiable desire to love as many people, animals, and nature's life forms as possible. They care for stray people, stray animals, and the gifts of nature, flowers, trees, and waters.

These spend their last money to buy food and clothes to clothe and feed other people. They model love for all. Regard for others and their needs consume their thoughts. They focus on how to make the lives of others better all the time. To do so is their joy.

Type 2

These survive their formative years in the fires of hell. They awaken from the brutal experiences of emotional and physical suffering as children and teens. Acts of violence were their normal experience growing up at home and school. The lingering effects of their traumatic and inhumane experiences produced lingering scars on their bodies and minds.

Having survived significant pain, they worked on accomplishing their own healing sufficient to assert themselves to help others surviving similar experiences to heal and prepare for love. They awakened to embody everything good they did not receive in their childhood and teen development. They commit their lives to love as many people, animals, and life forms of nature as possible.

Relationships of Types One and Two

Ones attract other ones for a relationship though they may feel called to love wounded others to wholeness. When ones join, both center on loving each other for the sake of shared joy. They mutually further empower each other at all times. Beyond their relationship, they focus on ways to provide love and care to others living without things that are necessary for life.

Twos attract other twos for a relationship. Because both have survived their physical and emotional wounds, when twos join, their first order of business is nurturing each other. They intentionally give to each other in ways that fulfill each other and help each other know emotional security.

Few are ones. Many more are twos. What happens if you do not have a sense of awakening to love? Is it possible to awaken to love?

If no clear awareness exists of being a one or a two, pass no judgment on yourself. Love begins with the desire to love and receive love. Loving life, loving self, loving others, and loving all life and creation serve as the prerequisite to receiving love.

We receive all the love we want when we give away all the love we need. Whether you are a one or two, want to be a one or a two, or simply do not know; love is your privilege and your choice. When we intentionally love because love is the right thing to do, we attract love.

I can hear you on the other side of the book saying, "Yes, but how?"

I am so glad you asked. This may prove to be simpler than you ever thought. Most things we believe hide from us actually hover around us out in the open. When we have eyes to see, we wonder how we missed it for so long.

Once our awakening comes to self – love comes, we see things we never noticed. Flower seeds grow flowers. Wow! Imagine that. Women and men make babies. Wow! The process works all over the world. The more we learn the more we grow and know.

We do not plant corn expecting to grow leather purses or shoes. We plant kernels of corn expecting tall stalks of corn with multiple ears of corn on each stalk. That is one seed producing one thousand.

When the awakened become love agricultural experts, we sow as many seeds of love as possible and guess what? We expect an abundant harvesting of love.

When the former energy of hurt and anger in us transforms into love, every person in our orbit receives the positive effect of the love energy love in us. When we intentionally sow love, we grow love.

What might happen if a group of ones got

together with a group of twos and other women and men dedicated to love? Could we intentionally focus our love on an issue, on a person, on a family, or on a nation and affect positive outcomes? The awakened to love do not hesitate. They declare a loud and resounding, "YES!"

Take a moment now to examine whether or not Chapter 5 has been of benefit to you and your developing understanding of love. Examine your personal thought by stepping inside the following questions and your own experience. Your truth will reveal itself.

Moments for Personal Thought

From reading Chapter 5, have you awakened to love? Please make notes to yourself asking the questions that might be helpful as your consider your response.

_____

_____
_____

_____

Are you a Type 1 or a Type 2? How have you sorted out your perception?
If you are gifted, what are your gifts? Do you think you could be awakened and not be aware of being

awakened?

_____

_____

_____

_____

Has Chapter 5 suggested to me ideas and activities that will help me establish or enhance a more practical understanding of what love is? What are they and what have you learned? Have I further learned what love is not?

_____

_____

_____

_____

What are my conclusions of love after reading Chapter 5?

_____

_____

_____

_____

What must I immediately stop doing because of reading Chapter 5?

_____

_____

_____

_____

What must I immediately begin to do after reading Chapter 5?

_____

_____

_____

Has the sense of my love mission changed since reading Chapter 5 or does my sense of my love mission remain the same?

What is my Love Mission? If it remains the same, reiterate it to reinforce to yourself. The more you affirm your mission to yourself, the more it becomes a real force in your life.

My Love Mission is

_____

_____

Chapter Six
So You Want to Experience Love

Let me be immediately clear, if you have the hunger, the craving and the desire for love, you must first become what you want to receive. You must first become the love you want and sow seeds of your love wherever you find opportunity. When the mid – 30's woman awakens to love and particularly self – love, she is ready to engage the process with a sense of urgency. Her urgency is not one of desperation. It is the determination to get it right and do it right.

Let's make another thing clear, love is not a thing found by looking and searching for it. Love may only be prepared for its coming. Another absolute, when love shows up, do not hesitate. Do not waste time. Be ready to move or love will move on without you.

Let's leave some tips on how to love in the ways that will attract love. The first tip is of what not to do. This is why most churches fail in the mission Jesus left for the beloved community do. Jesus said and I paraphrase, "Go love people (Matthew 28 vss 19 – 20)." The church misses the point by sitting in boxes expecting people to show up when none there invite anyone or give them reason to come.

People with a heart for love are not sitting idly by hoping someone will incidentally show up. No, they show up where people are with a friendly face, a loving heart, and an engaging personality. These do not wait for others to speak first. They speak first.

Tip Number One – Self – Love

The notion of self – love scares many people because their religions teach them that self – love is conceit, pride and arrogance. Nothing could be further from the truth.

The Judeo – Christian Context affirms self - love by commandment in the Torah – Hebrew Bible (Deuteronomy 6 vs 5 – Reiterated in Deuteronomy 10 vs 12 and Deuteronomy 30 vs 6) and the Gospel (Matthew 22 vss 36 – 40 – Reiterated in Luke 10 vs 27).

Love's Order is Love God, Love Self, and Loves others as you love yourself. It is a Love Trifecta. We cannot love others until we have properly loved ourselves. Them we have a reference for how to give love and love others, the same way we want loved.

Self – Love is an act of love.

Tip Number 2 – Affirm the Positive

While nothing is absolute, this works. The moment you are meeting someone for the first time, size him or her up quickly and discover something positive you can affirm. You can say, "I really like your shoes. Where did you get them?"

When they begin to tell you more than you ask, observe their body language. You may be the first person to show them a kind word in a long time. Many people are hungry for someone to notice them, affirm them, and show them the love of care, essentially give them attention.

This may feel uncomfortable and unnatural at first and that you are making stuff up. You are not. You are intentionally connecting with others in polite ways that affirm and empower them. Keep loving people. Keep affirming people. Keep empowering people until it becomes natural. Think about it. You know you enjoy it when someone affirms you.

Affirming others is an act of love. It is an act of the willful intention to create the experience of joy in another or others.

Tip Number 3 – Express Interest

People with a passion for love and for loving are not boring. No one wants to experience boredom. When you engage someone, have something to say. Have some enthusiasm in your voice. Let your face reveal you feel good to notice them and to share with them.

Your next move is to ask a question. Ask the person, "How do you feel or how are you feeling today?" Say to them, "You look energized and ready to take on the world. What's your secret?"

Hardly anyone asks that question unless acquaintances or close. People are hungry to feel someone else is genuinely interested in them. Express interest through the asking of questions.

Expressing interest in others is an act of love they may feel good about for days. You are someone that took time to show interest.

Tip Number 4 - Be a Good Listener

When you notice someone seems a bit down, do not hesitate to express concern. Ask if the person would like to talk. Find a place to sit with them. Listen with your heart.

Do not offer to fix the situation. Simply listen without judgment. If asked what you would do, do not make anything up. Ask the person what they think is the best way for everything to work out for them. They know their answers. They simply need to feel cared for at the moment and not feel alone.

Being present with a loving heart without judgment is an act of love.

Tip Number 5 – Volunteer

Volunteer at a Hospital for Veterans or Children, a Senior Care Center, or a homeless shelter. Take your children with you if appropriate. Let your children see you love by example.

Take a moment to be with people that feel forgotten. Develop the gift for helping people feel relevant whatever their circumstance. When your children observe you do this. They will be inspired like mom. Mom loves people.

Serving people that feel forgotten is an act of love. You can feel good about your responsible act of love.

Tip Number 6 – Express Gratitude

Expressing gratitude for love upon waking every morning is an experience of love and beauty. It is a most beautiful way of expressing how we feel inside to the universe for its gifts and expressing how we feel about and to the people whose love we share, enjoy, and consistently experience.

The consistent expression of gratitude provides more and more opportunity to be grateful for more. Every morning you wake and become conscious, be thankful for the special souls it is your privilege to love and your privilege to share their love.

Expressing Gratitude is an act of love.

Tip Number 7 – Be Prepared for Love

When your love harvest comes, that is not the time to say I am scared. I do not know what to do. Love will believe you and offer itself to another that is ready.

When you work hard every day on loving yourself, your family and others by intention, you prepare for the coming of intimate love. When intimate love arrives, you may feel shaken to your core asking, "What do I do now?"

What you have worked hard to prepare for its

arrival and hoped for is now real and in your presence. This is not the time to get gun shy. It is time to do the adult thing, assert yourself. You are ready. You are prepared. You know what to do.

Now is your time. Go love. Cash in your chips for love. Burn your bridges for love. Live and love as if you are running out of time. You are, so get busy loving love.

Being prepared for love is an act of love.

Take a moment now to examine whether or not Chapter 6 has been of benefit to you and your developing understanding of love. Examine your personal thought by stepping inside the following questions and your own experience. Your truth will reveal itself.

Moments for Personal Thought

Do I hunger for love, crave love, and desire love? If I say yes, am I willing to do what is necessary to attract the love I hunger for, crave and desire?

_____

_____

_____

_____

Am I clear on the idea, I must first become love to attract love into my life? Am I clear on how that works?

_____

_____

_____

_____

I desire love with a sense of urgency. Does my current behavior say that I desire love with a sense of urgency?

_____

_____

_____

_____

Do I make the same mistake many churches make expecting people to show up without invitation and without preparation for their arrival? Do I just expect love to show up without me doing anything? If I do, why do I think that.

_____

_____

_____

_____

How do I really feel about self - love? Is it right to put
oneself before others? Do I in respect myself or love
myself? Can I express gratitude and prepare myself for
love? Do I really want love in my life? Can I be honest
with myself?

_____

_____

_____

_____

Can I do the others tips? Will they work for me? Can I
affirm the positive and express interest in someone I
just met? How will they feel about it? Can I be a good
listener? Can I volunteer? Can I demonstrate care?

_____

_____

_____

_____

Has the sense of my love mission changed since
reading Chapter 6 or does my sense of my love
mission remain the same?

What is my Love Mission? If it remains the same, reiterate it to reinforce to yourself. The more you affirm your mission to yourself, the more it becomes a real force in your life.

My Love Mission is

_____

_____

The Conclusion

I feel your heart with my heart. Your love is unconditional, so strong and can penetrate in every unloved part. *~Daniela Babun*

While what has been shared is not the final word on love, it accomplishes the revealing of what love is and what love is not for the mid – 30's woman. Tired of hurting over what happened earlier in her life, she decides to do the most adult thing she has ever done in her life. She decides to love herself and leave her arrested development behind. She will now emotionally evolve into the adult woman that she is by chronological age. She assumes responsibility for her past, her present, and her future.

She elects to turn all her energies into her own personal self – development. She loves herself enough that she will allow no one to frustrate her purpose. She has discovered that living in the past gets her left behind. She is finished with that.

If she is to move on, she must help herself with the power of her own decision to be self – determining. The past will no longer be a power to control her and keep her bound in an emotional prison. She claims her personal power to be the focus of her purpose to love and come alive. She knows what happened to her had absolutely nothing to do with her.

She will get the help she needs to heal. She will transform her anger and depression into love and will begin to look out for other women that may yet be suffering over what happened to them decades ago or weeks ago. She knows the experience of suffering and seeks to alleviate the suffering of others where it is within her power to do so.

She will do what is necessary to become first the love she wants to attract into her life. She will give away all the love she wants to get all the love she needs. She will do the due diligence personal work necessary to attract the love she hungers for, craves and desires. She will no longer be in her own way. She has clarity. People bring the right energy into her space or she will allow them to be anywhere she is not.

What Love Is Not

Love is not acting out in violence on children, helpless girl children or women soldiers. Love is not rape. Love is not inflicting harm upon anyone causing them to live with post-traumatic stress disorder PTSD.

While we did not deal with this here, there are cultures living with a collective PTSD. Muslims and Jews live with the tragedies of their past suffering.

Native Americans and African Americans live with a collective Cultural PTSD. Only when we culturally awaken to self–love, as described in this book will we evolve beyond our pain filled and suffering pasts.

Love is not ignoring our suffering or the suffering of any. Where any of us suffer, our species suffers. We can do better than the threats of war and watching more than 3 billion people suffer the indignity of poverty.

What Love Is

Love is the capacity to be present with a loving caring heart without the necessity to be judgmental. Love is the burning desire to give to others in such a way they are liberated from their pain and suffering and empowered to live freely and determine their new path to love and new life.

Love is also the desire to attract fulfilling love and all its accompaniments into one's life. The desire to be love, live love, and experience love is a significant human imperative. When we achieve and experience love, humans can do anything.

Love is realizing it is necessary to become what we want to receive. Love is accepting our lives as they are and building the life we want to live on the foundations of our pain and suffering. Many mid – 30's women experiencing the cruel indignity of rape as small children awaken to acknowledge their pain and suffering become redemptive when transformed to love with purpose.

Love is working very hard to alleviate suffering in the experience of others as much as is in us possible. We know pain and suffering and want no one to go through what we have survived. In spite of our pain and suffering, on our awakening to love, in a strange way only love realized can produce, all our pain and suffering seems worth it to have arrived at the point we attract more love into our lives than we ever imagined possible.

To this end, *Let's Talk About Love – a Guide to Love and Come Alive for the Awakening Mid- 30's Woman Living with PTSD resulting from Sexual Violence while a child* is dedicated. We are all in this together. We have the power and the possibility to build a better world one awakened woman or man to self-love and one relationship at a time. All my hopes and prayers are that you are committed to the shared journey. We all need each other. What we sow together, we grow together.

Are your ready to love, as you have never sown love before? Did I hear you say yes? Then let us get busy. We have work to do.

Take a moment now to examine whether or not the Conclusion has been of benefit to you and your developing understanding of love. Examine your personal thought by stepping inside the following questions and your own experience. Your truth will reveal itself.

Moments for Personal Thought

Do you now have a clearer perspective on what love is and what love is not?

_____

_____

_____

Have you developed a greater appreciation for women because you have read *Let's Talk About Love – a Guide to Love and Come Alive for the Awakening Mid- 30's Woman Living with PTSD resulting from Sexual Violence while a child?*

_____

_____

_____

Have you arrived a clear understanding of your Love Mission? Can you state your love mission in one clear sentence?

_____

_____

_____

What adjustments have you discovered necessary to develop a more quality self – love and love for others?

_____

_____

_____

Have you awakened to love?

_____

_____

_____

_____

A Final Thought

Love is the most significant teacher and motivation any of us can experience in our lives. Love drives us every day. It is the most powerful invisible and intangible force existing in the world.

Actually, what is love? The question examined in *Let's Talk About Love – a Guide to Love and Come Alive for the Awakening Mid- 30's Woman Living with PTSD resulting from Sexual Violence while a child* will continue as long as there is human consciousness and human presence on Earth.

Where does Love come from? Is it like calcium in our teeth or iron in our blood? Could it be like the double helix in our DNA? What brings love to life? How would we know if we never received proper education and instruction while growing up from those designed to love us!

Love's magnificence shines bright like the sun and the moon. It can prompt the presence of feeling from ecstasy to torment. Somewhere inside us, love integrates itself into us and we were born to love and experience love and experience love.

Through women and men, love charts its own course to find those women and men prepared to receive love. Love knows no limits or boundaries of color, culture, class, religion, politics or worldviews. Love will dwell where love chooses. Love is as necessary for human life to be meaningful as water, air, food, clothes, housing, and work.

The mesmerizing attraction of love compels us. We humans are obsessed with love, its accompanying sexual energy, and our desire for an intimate other demands our attention.

I know love exists in our DNA. I just cannot prove it, yet. My investigation continues.

Annemarie Van Rooyen
Poet, Author, and Accountant

In 2019, Annemarie Van Rooyen and Oscar Crawford will collaborate and co – author the sequel to Let's Talk About Love.

APPENDIX
New Opportunities for Love

When we have faced the terrors of honoring our unresolved past hurts and disappointments, honored our emotional anger, honored our PTSD, admitted the need to heal, transformed our anger energy into love energy, forgiven all that have caused us harm and liberated ourselves to love and come alive; we have new opportunities to love. How can we discover what those new opportunities are?

West African wisdom says we are limited to begin where we find ourselves. We start right where we are. Where are we? We are where we experience our physical and emotional pain and that is exactly where we begin to recover, renew, and restore ourselves.

Chinese wisdom philosopher Lao Tzu taught that no matter how far you must go on your journey, you must begin your journey. His famous line says, "The journey of 1,000 miles begins with a single step." The combined wisdom of east and west makes clear that the journey to new opportunities for love must begin within us and from there we take the first step to begin our journey into love.

The first step we must take is intentionally

showing ourselves love to begin to feel good. Feeling good is important. This encourages us to continue producing work to reproduce what feels good to continue feeling good. What do we enjoy doing that makes us feel good? Whatever that is, we should begin to do it and do it regularly.

This can include writing in a journal. It can include spending time in nature. It can mean engaging a new learning activity. It can mean listening to favorite inspiring music. It can be spending time with a favorite loved one. It could be spending time in meditation or practicing spirituality.

This can include going to the gym, going for a run, lifting weights, or going for a walk. It can mean enjoying a full body massage. It can mean eating your favorite meal. It can mean practicing yoga. It can mean making love with your lover.

After giving ourselves love that we can feel, the next step in new opportunities to love is reaching beyond ourselves to love others. Begin with showing love to immediate family and closest friends. The most effective way to do this is to spend intentional time with people you care about and that are important to you. You want them to know how you feel about them.

Just being present demonstrates love and care.

Most of us most of the time want to be loved by others that care about us. We feel accepted and affirmed when someone wants to spend time with us. We feel good when someone loves us, cares about us, and does not judge us.

Another solid way to show love to others is to help people in need do something they cannot do for themselves. Going to shop for food for someone that cannot is a major help. Cleaning someone's house or apartment that cannot is a huge help. Cooking for someone and preparing her or his meals is a big help.

These new opportunities for loving others and ourselves follow working through our personal pain. When we keep our eye on recovery, renewal, and restoration, new opportunities to love will find us.

This functional practice to developing beyond our pain provides an opportunity to live consciously in the present to make responsible choices to feel good and affirm our humanity. Life will now open to us new opportunities to love we may never have dreamed.

Man, How Do You Do It?

I love food, all types of food. I love Korean food, Japanese, Italian, and French. In Australia, we do not have a distinctive Australian food, so we have food from everywhere all around the world. We are very multicultural, so we grew up with lots of different types of food. ~Hugh Jackman

There were Long Ones, Short Ones, Tall Ones, Brown Ones, Black Ones, Round Ones, Big Ones; they came all. ~War

Throughout my adult life and career, I have worked with women as individuals, as groups, and as teams. 90% of the people I have worked with have been women. I did not choose this component of my career. This was not a chosen career and I cannot tell you this was my life plan. The great power of the universe made this choice for me and prepared me to carry it out.

It has been my service privilege to send women to participate and contribute to state, national, and international events and activities empowering women. I found myself in the right place at the right time to appoint women to opportunities and positions previously denied them and previously held only by men.

Men often asked me, "Man, how do you do it? How do you stand to be around so many women all the time? That would drive me crazy. I just could not do it." I never understood how an adult man could ask another adult man this question.

Laguna Beach California

In California on business, a group of corporate colleagues and I are on a work trip in Orange County. During some down time, we made our way to Laguna Beach. I could not wait to get there. My frequency climbs. I feel good.   I am excited about the people I will meet and get to know. I am like Casper, the Friendly Ghost. I want to make new friends, and build new relationships.

When we arrived, I was in earth heaven. I was ready to see and have others see me. To my amazement, my traveling companions experience awe over the stilted houses hanging off the side of the mountains looking down on the beach. High-end cars put them in a trance. They all simply looked at me and said in essential unison, "Don't hate. We all get excited about different things."

I left them making my way to the beach losing clothes with every step I took. I found myself transcending lucid dreaming in the sunlight as I walked and appreciated lovers of the sun.

A song from the past began to play in my mind. I danced as I walked and heard the music in my head. I am alive in a perfect moment. Spill the Wine by War on my internal turntable. I heard these lyrics.

"But there I was, I was taken to a place, the hall of the mountain kings
I stood high upon a mountain top, naked to the world
In front of every kind of girl, There were Long Ones, Short Ones, Tall Ones, Brown Ones, Black Ones, Round Ones, Big Ones; they came all.

Out of the middle came a lady
She whispered in my ear something crazy
She said: Spill the wine and take that pearl, Spill the wine and take that pearl
Spill the wine and take that pearl, Spill the wine and take that pearl"

An energy force moved me to observe a beautiful caramel woman observing me. She had noticed I looked like I was in another dimensional space.

She touched me and said, "I do not know where you are but I would love to go with you." We smiled to each other experiencing the kind of love-filled moment that lasts for an eternity looking at each other as she walked away.

In the moment, I am complete. I need nothing. I

sat on the sand looking back at my strewn clothes. When the one that had touched me returned, she had collected my clothes and said to me, "You are probably going to need these later."

I thanked her as she gave them to me. She asked if she could join me. I nodded yes.

We sat there together just looking out over the Pacific Ocean for hours without saying a word. When it was time for her to go, she leaned in to kiss me behind my left ear. She whispered, "Thank you."

I looked into her eyes without saying anything. She felt my question. She whispered again, "Thank you for allowing me to be free with you. You asked nothing of me. It was refreshing."

As she walked away, I felt the sensation of extreme gratitude. I did until the sensation ended. I heard voices calling my name. My colleagues found me. They looked at me as if they never saw a naked man before. The call came for our return to the business conference table. They could not return without me. Somewhere in my clothes lay a necessary key.

"Who was that?" One of them asked. "Did you get her number? Does she have friends?"

I said, "I do not know, no, and I do not know."

How to Love and Respect Women

The report God made the first man is a continuing discussion. Who gave birth to the rest is not. ~Magi Aata

The key to human survival lies in humanity learning to respect and value women. Mark Twain once commented, "What, sir, would the people of the Earth be without woman?" His response to his own question was, "They would be scarce, sir, almighty scarce."

Women have survived physical and emotional trauma at the hands of males from the beginning of prehistory to the present. The film project "Coming of the Red Rain" dramatizes this uncivilized behavior of males is consistent in any era.

Four prehistoric males return from a hunt carrying the animal they have killed. It is food for their village. The scent of a young woman distracts them. They drop former prey for new prey.

They track the woman's scent and surround her. They subdue her and then fight over who will have her first. They drag her to a cave. The last man standing will sexually brutalize her first and others will follow in turn of their fall. When they finish they leave her bloodied, bruised, and battered. They are back to business as usual.

What is the difference between the behavior of these four prehistoric males and the behavior of four contemporary males in a club on a weekend night that drug a woman's drink and drag her to a cave called hotel. When they finish they leave her bloodied, bruised, and battered. They are back to business as usual.

Women are valuable to life and not a commodity for selling products or being the products of sex trafficking, slavery, pornography (Huffington Post) or any other commercially exploitive industry. Women are valuable because there is no human life without women. The best of us and the worst of us have arrived at life through the belly womb of a woman. There are no exceptions.

The better amongst us seek to bring joy to the women in our lives. The smile alone of the right woman is more valuable than money. The smile affirms life and empowers life to further development.

Men and women respect and value women when love, respect, and honor for women are normative human behaviors, the rule and not the exception. Women deserve, as do all other humans, to live without fear of the threat of intimidation, violence, or exploitation. Where women are present, life energy powers action.

Women free to live out their own faith and values inspire creativity by their presence. Women free to make sexual choices in their own interests without threat or intimidation give birth to a better world.

If you love and honor women, you are committed to making the world a better place for women and all women influence. Do this by daily committing to honor and respect women with your best gifts of love and care. When you do, watch women give themselves to the healing of our world.

How to Find Your Beauty through Self - Appreciation

This article will demonstrate the benefits of implementing self-appreciation as an intentional activity in daily life for good mental and physical health. How is that people can look at other people, places, things, and declare them beautiful but never quite manage to apply ideas of beauty to themselves? The answer is because too few have ever been taught how to or had the behavior modeled for them to apply.

People tend to see beauty only in other people, places, and things beyond themselves. How different might people be if taught beauty must be part of them to recognize it beyond themselves in others and other things? Might that awareness bring with it the capacity for enhanced self-appreciation?

Self - Appreciation

Self - appreciation is the capacity to perceive, feel, and express authentic positive regard for self as a unique expression of life with infinite possibilities. David, King of Ancient Israel may have summed up self - appreciation best in Psalms 139 vs. 14. Aware of the majesty and beauty of his own creation from the mind and heart of unseen hands made this powerful comment one for the ages.

He said and I paraphrase, "I am so well made I am awesome. My soul well knows that I am awesome because awesome is the Creator's works." I am awesome! You are awesome! We are all awesome!

Consequences of the Lack of Self - Appreciation

Charles Dickens' Classic, A Tale of Two Cities begins with the words, "It was the best of times, it was the worst of times. It was the season of light. It was the season of darkness."

Dickens describes a time not so very different from our own. For some, it is the best of times and they are too few. For some, it is the worst of times and they are too many. Many consider this is the age of disappointment. Born to live the dream of ancestors where everything seemed possible, something has gone terribly wrong.

In the age of disappointment, people require blaming something or someone. It is the economy's fault. It is the President's fault. It is the opposition party's fault. It is the rich's fault. It is the poor's fault. Blame always finds an object for its negative affection.

Disappointment unmanaged for too long can become depression. Depression unmanaged for too long can become despair. Despair that does not seek help can drown in mental illness. These are but of few of the negative consequences of the lack of self - appreciation.

Advantages of Self – Appreciation

The primary advantage of self- appreciation is clarity. Clarity allows people to look at newborn babies, beautiful flowers, art, and not see them as something of beauty detached from them but as reflections of their inner sense of self.

Clarity allows for the pursuit of goals, wants, and desires to emerge from the inner motivation of personal interests. There exists minimal to no need to keep up with the Jones to do what they do or have what they have. People with clarity want what they want because they are clear about what they want.

Process for Achieving Self - Appreciation

In my mid - 30's, I discovered my personal beauty. It dawned on me that I recognized beauty in women, in children, in nature, in written words, in pictures, in art, in songs, and in film because beauty is alive in me. That is a personal game changer.

The light bulb just came on. If I could recognize

beauty outside me, it had to be in me. It was a turning point. My ability to love and respect others and myself sharply increased.

This can work with intention. When there is a moment, listen to Joe Cocker's song, "You are so beautiful to me" as if you are singing the song to yourself. Really feel your beauty as if you are looking at yourself through the eyes of your own intense love for the first time.

If it takes a bit of practice, that is OK. Look through the eyes of the persons that have loved you most in your life, really loved you. On the other hand, look through the eyes of your favorite pet that adored you. See and sense what they saw when looking up at you with eyes forever adoring you.

You will feel a bit of what beauty is really trying to offer us all, a bit more reason to loving of our self and others. Self - appreciation is good medicine for mental and physical health.

Women That Understand Men Do These Things Every Time

Women that understand men do these things every time. This woman loves herself. She knows her worth. She knows what she wants. She likes men and enjoys being the woman that appeals to them. She knows how to get what she wants.

Whatever it takes, she makes her focused interests known subtly, assertively or aggressively. She immediately finds something to affirm in the man who interests her. She touches him when close enough to communicate levels of interests and intention.

The Conscious Woman

The conscious woman does not seek permission to be who she is, to share her interests, or to make her own decisions. She knows what she wants and learns ways to get what she wants. She studies people. She studies men. She studies other women.

In her pursuit of the one who will share her heart song of life and love for a lifetime, she screens many. She filters out the weak and immature. She is not interested in the flash of accessories or cash. She is interested in the one who does not need the affirmation of the crowd to be secure within his own person. She seeks to form a loving and productive connection that can stand the test of time. She is developed and unique. Her choice must be also.

Appealing to Men in the Now

Her study of men has taught her that men live in the emotional moment of now where women are concerned. Men have many available choices among females. Some are available much too easy and are soon discarded. The woman who wants a man's attention over time must engage a man where he feels.

That begins with his ego. Appeal to his ego and get his attention. Appeal to his heart starved for love wrapped in sexy feminine intelligence and he will hunger for connection beyond his immediate biology. He will want his biology managed with love and care regularly but his desire for that with a trustworthy sexy feminine intelligence wrapped in beautiful skin generates the appeal he will want to connect with long term.

Not Afraid to Act

She is not afraid to act. When she identifies a target, she is a no holds barred woman. She will get the attention of the man in her sights by her subtlety, by her aggressive nature or by being outright aggressive, whatever it takes.

This can require a simple act of clumsy to test

his helping reflex. It can require a more direct approach to the expression of interest. Extreme action reveals a once in a lifetime offer indicating visions of possibilities unavailable anywhere else in any other. She is a free and adult woman giving no thought to what others think. She is a woman with clarity of mission.

Excellent Communicator and Good Investment

She communicates when she is ready for partnership in the venture of long-term love. She communicates clearly her preparedness to be a woman in love in full expression. She is a good investment because she is industrious by nature. She knows she is a great deal.

Her expectations are clear. Live with her faithfully and honestly and she opens her all to you to your delight to your mutually shared engagement and experience in the mysteries of love. Do not and she will return you where she found you. Women that understand men do these things every time.

10 Personal Development Books for Recommended Reading

You Can Heal Your Life
by Louise Hay

Women That Love Too Much
by Robin Norwood

I Never Knew I Had a Choice
by Corey and Corey

The Four Agreements
by Don Miguel Ruiz

A Return to Love
by Marianne Williamson

Soul Mates
by Thomas Moore

The Secret
by Rhonda Byrne

Psycho – Cybernetics
by Dr. Maxwell Maltz

How to Win Friends and Influence People
by Dale Carnegie

The Power of Your Subconscious Mind
by Dr. Joseph Murphy

Available on Amazon by the Author

Fishers of Men
What Single Woman Should Know
About When Searching for Husbands

Receive FREE

NEGOTIATED RELATIONSHIPS

How to Strategies to Achieve Functional and
Productive Outcomes in Personal and Professional
Relationships

When you request the
Let's Talk About Love Newsletter
EMAIL YOUR REQUEST to
info@oscarcrawfordmedia.com

ABOUT THE AUTHOR

Oscar Crawford writes fiction and non - fiction works focused on the end of sexual and domestic violence, and poverty among women and children. Committed to helping hurting people heal and prepare for love, he works with spiritual partners to build a better world, one relationship at a time.

Travel in 30 states in the U. S. and 20 nations from Europe to Asia, he has interviewed thousands of women and listened to their dating and mating rituals, their triumphs and their disappointments. He has earned graduate degrees from the Methodist Theological School in Ohio and the University of Phoenix in Arizona.

He is the author of the fiction titles Tainted Money, ReVengeance, Behind the Waterfall, the Lady with the Slanted Halo, and Burning Flame. Non – fiction titles include Fishers of Men: What Single Women Need to Know When Searching for Husbands, Negotiated Relationships: How to Strategies to Achieve Functional and Productive Outcomes in Personal and Professional Relationships, Living Christian in an Unchristian World, and a content creator for print and online media delivering information, inspiration, and entertainment.

Oscar descends from four generations of educators and clergy. He lives with wife, retired social worker and writer, Bonnie in Chandler, Arizona. They share six children, seventeen grandchildren, and six great grandchildren.

He is an award winning author and commissioned a Kentucky Colonel by Governor Julian Carroll and the recipient of the World Humanitarian Service Award by the Family Federation for World Peace and Unification.

LET

www.ingramcontent.com/pod-product-compliance
Lightning Source LLC
Chambersburg PA
CBHW071137280326
41935CB00010B/1260